Oh Dear Tree

Debbie Wood

Copyright © 2024 by Debbie Wood

All rights reserved.
No part of this book may be reproduced or used in any manner without written permission of the copyright owner except for the use of quotations in a book review.

First paperback edition 2024

Written by Debbie Wood
Illustrated by Millie Moth

978-1-80541-511-4 (paperback)
978-1-80541-512-1 (ebook)

Tree loved his little world.

He loved the little bees buzzing about and the beautiful fluttery butterflies.

His coat of green leaves made him so proud.

That warming feeling as the sun shone down on his branches was just perfect.

He felt so happy every day.

Then one day, things started to change.

He lost his coat of green leaves which made him feel so sad.

He started to feel very lonely.

Where were his friends, the fluttery butterflies and the buzzy bees?

Even his warming friend, the sun, didn't come out to play anymore.

One day it all got too much and he let out big sobs of sadness.

Bird heard Tree's sobs,
"Oh Dear Tree!
What could the matter be?"

With big sobs, Tree cried,
"Just look at me, I'm all bare.
My coat of green leaves,
it's all.....gone!"

"Oh Dear Tree!
Where could it be?
Don't worry, I'll solve the mystery."
Wheeeeeee! And off he flew.

A little later, Bird flew back.

"I'm so sorry Tree,
I didn't find your coat of green leaves.
But I did find leaves of all different colours,
reds, oranges, browns and yellows.
All dancing in the wind.
Falling to the ground.
They were very beautiful."

Tree thought for a while.
"Hmmm, that does sound very beautiful.
I would like to see that."
He slowly started to smile.

But the smile soon changed to sadness.

Bird heard Tree's sobs,
"Oh Dear Tree!
What could the matter be?"

With bigger sobs, Tree cried,
"The children...they have gone too.
They used to paddle barefoot in the stream here."

"Oh Dear Tree!
Where could they be?
Don't worry I'll solve the mystery."
Wheeeeeee! And off he flew.

A little later, Bird flew back.

"I'm so sorry Tree, I didn't find the children paddling barefoot in the stream. But I did find giggly, happy, children wrapped up in wellies and waterproofs, jumping in muddy puddles from the rain. It was very beautiful."

Tree thought for a while. "Hmmm that does sound very beautiful. I would like to see that." He slowly started to smile.

But the smile soon changed to sadness.
Bird heard Tree's sobs,
"Oh Dear Tree!
What could the matter be?"

With even bigger sobs, Tree cried,
"The rainbow of colour from the flowers...it's all gone!"

"Oh Dear Tree,
Where could it be?
Don't worry, I'll solve the mystery."
Wheeeeeee! And off he flew.

A little later, Bird flew back.

"I'm so sorry Tree,
I didn't find the rainbow of colour
from the flowers.
But I did find lots of delicious berries,
ripe and ready for a yummy crumble.
It was very beautiful."

Tree thought for a while.
"Hmmm, that does sound very beautiful.
I would like to see that."
He slowly started to smile.

But the smile soon changed to sadness.
Bird heard Tree's sobs,
"Oh Dear Tree!
What could the matter be!"

With the biggest sobs, Tree cried,
"The fluttery butterflies and the buzzy bees.
They've all...gone!"

"Oh Dear Tree,
Where could they be?
Don't worry, I'll solve the mystery."
Wheeeeeee! And off he flew.

A little later, Bird flew back.

"I'm so sorry Tree,
I didn't find the fluttery butterflies and the buzzy bees.
But I did find lots of woodland creatures, scurrying about the woods collecting nuts.
It was very beautiful."

Tree and Bird sat silently for a moment.
Just thinking.
Owl had been watching and listening all day.
Down he flew to share his wisdom.

"Tree, Bird...

You might not find the rainbow of colour in the flowers...

Or the fluttery butterflies and buzzy bees...

Or the barefoot children paddling in the stream...

And Tree, it may be a little while before you find your coat of green leaves too...

But that's okay.

"It's okay because today we can find delicious berries ready for a crumble...

And beautiful leaves dancing in the air...

We can find woodland animals collecting food from around the forest floor...

And children happily stamping and splashing in the muddy puddles...

All those things are just as beautiful.

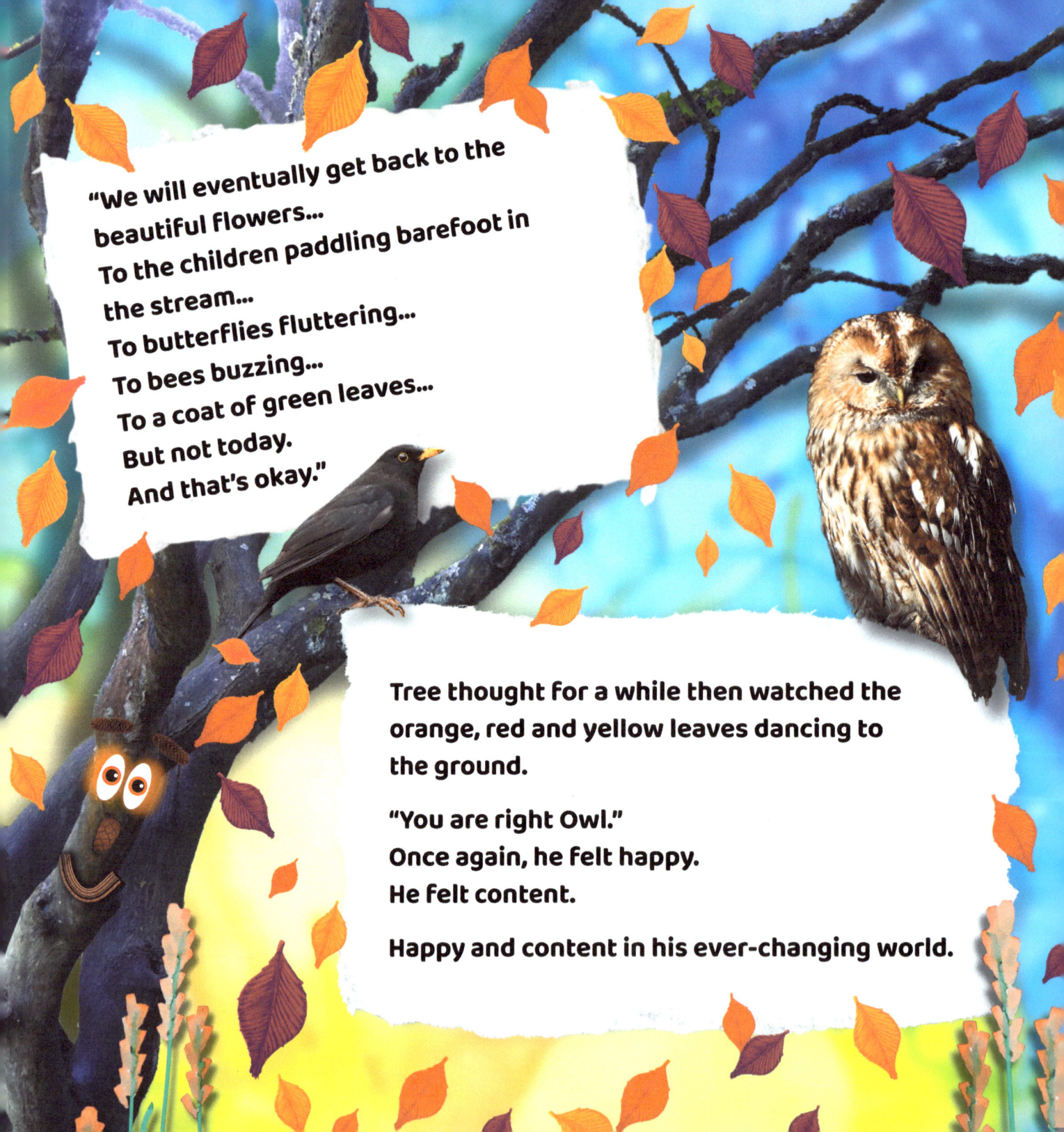

"We will eventually get back to the beautiful flowers...
To the children paddling barefoot in the stream...
To butterflies fluttering...
To bees buzzing...
To a coat of green leaves...
But not today.
And that's okay."

Tree thought for a while then watched the orange, red and yellow leaves dancing to the ground.

"You are right Owl."
Once again, he felt happy.
He felt content.

Happy and content in his ever-changing world.

About the Author

Hello you lovely people. Firstly a big thank you for supporting me by buying this book. A dream for me has definitely come true!

Who would have known a few ideas scribbled down in lockdown would lead to working with my amazing illustrator Karen and then Publishing Push to create "Oh Dear Tree."

I am forever grateful to you all. ❤️

I trained as an Early Years Teacher back in 1998 and have a passion for all things nature-based. I believe that children's discovery and exploration of the natural world is very important. I am currently an outdoor-based childminder, working in the beautiful Peak District, where our adventures develop imagination, curiosity, resilience and a deep respect for our wonderful world. 🙂

Sharing stories is one of our favourite things to do, especially under the trees. Go! Take this book out to the woods and enjoy. 🌳

Website: www.debbie-wood-author.co.uk

Email: debbiejwood26@gmail.com

Facebook: rainbows and puddles books

Instagram: rainbows_and_puddles_books

About the Illustrator

My name is Karen Johnson and I'm the Derby-based artist behind Millie Moth. I created the pictures featured in this story using digital collages which use a combination of my paintings, drawings and photographic images. My work is full of colour and I aim to convey the happiness I feel when I'm around flowers and foliage. There is such a wealth of life in every small growing space and I try to capture that beauty and vigour by injecting a little wildness and joy into everything I work on.

Website: milliemoth.com

Email: milliemothdesigns@gmail.com

Instagram: @millie.moth

www.ingramcontent.com/pod-product-compliance
Lightning Source LLC
Chambersburg PA
CBHW041527070526
44585CB00002B/108